PRAISE FOR
THE MARRIAGE SERIES

We often hear that the institution of marriage is suffering. But there is good news, too! By submitting their relationships to God and seeking out the right resources, married couples can know what it means to truly *thrive*. That's what Focus on the Family's Marriage Series is all about. Whether you're in a small group, a mentoring relationship, or you just want to study as a couple, this series can transform your marriage for the better.

Jim Daly
President, Focus on the Family

A strong marriage is the cornerstone of a strong home, and a strong home is the cornerstone of strong churches and communities, as well as our nation. These Bible studies cover the pertinent areas of making marriages thrive, and I highly recommend them whether you are newly married or seasoned.

Dr. Tony Evans
Senior Pastor, Oak Cliff Bible Fellowship
Author, *Kingdom Man* and *Kingdom Woman*

Marriage is an amazing adventure—filled with excitement, joy and challenges. Focus on the Family's Marriage Series examines God's gift of marriage in all of its wonderful dimensions. I consider it a privilege to be involved with this important set of relationship-strengthening resources.

Dr. Greg Smalley
Vice President, Family Ministries, Focus on the Family

In a day and age where the covenant of marriage is so quickly tossed aside in the name of incompatibility and irreconcilable differences, a marriage Bible study that is both inspirational and practical is desperately needed. The Focus on the Family Marriage Series is what couples are seeking. I give my highest recommendation to this Bible study series that has the potential to dramatically impact and improve marriages today. Marriage is not so much about finding the right partner as it is about being the right partner. These studies give wonderful biblical teaching for helping those who want to learn the beautiful art of being and becoming all that God intends in their marriage.

Lysa TerKeurst

President, Proverbs 31 Ministries
Author, *Capture Her Heart; Capture His Heart,*
and the *New York Times* Bestsellers *Made to Crave* and *Unglued*

The Focus on the Family Marriage Series is just what the doctor ordered: It's timely and timeless—chock-full of grounded information and tools every couple can put into practice immediately. You won't want to miss out on this incredible resource.

Drs. Les & Leslie Parrott

Authors, *Saving Your Marriage Before It Starts*

In my 31 years as a pastor, I've officiated at hundreds of weddings. Unfortunately, many of those unions failed. I only wish the Focus on the Family Marriage Series had been available to me during those years. What a marvelous tool you as pastors and Christian leaders have at your disposal. I encourage you to use it to assist those you serve in building successful, healthy marriages.

H.B. London, Jr.

Pastor to Pastors Emeritus, Focus on the Family

This marriage study series is pure Focus on the Family—reliable, biblically sound and dedicated to reestablishing family values in today's society. This series will no doubt help a multitude of couples strengthen their relationship, not only with each other, but also with God, the creator of marriage itself.

Bruce Wilkinson
Author, *Secrets of the Vine, A Life God Rewards,
Dream Giver* and the *New York Times* Bestseller *The Prayer of Jabez*

Looking for a prescription for a better marriage? You'll enjoy this timely and practical series!

Dr. Kevin Leman
Bestselling Author, *Sheet Music: Uncovering the Secrets of
Sexual Intimacy in Marriage*

THE MARRIAGE SERIES

The Passionate Marriage

EXPLORE. REFLECT. UNITE.

BETHANYHOUSE
a division of Baker Publishing Group
Minneapolis, Minnesota

© 2014 Focus on the Family

Published by Bethany House Publishers
11400 Hampshire Avenue South
Bloomington, Minnesota 55438
www.bethanyhouse.com

Bethany House Publishers is a division of
Baker Publishing Group, Grand Rapids, Michigan
www.bakerpublishinggroup.com

Printed in the United States of America

All rights reserved. No part of this publication may be reproduced, stored in a retrieval system or transmitted in any form or by any means—for example, electronic, photocopy, recording—without the prior written permission of the publisher. The only exception is brief quotations in printed reviews.

Library of Congress Cataloging-in-Publication Data is on file at the Library of Congress, Washington, DC.

All Scripture quotations, unless otherwise indicated, are taken from the *Holy Bible, New International Version®. NIV®* Copyright © 1973, 1978, 1984 by Biblica, Inc.™ Used by permission of Zondervan. All rights reserved worldwide. www.zondervan.com The "NIV" and "New International Version" are trademarks registered in the United States Patents and Trademark Office by Biblica, Inc.™

Focus on the Family is a global Christian ministry dedicated to helping families thrive. They provide help and resources for couples to build healthy marriages that reflect God's design and for parents to raise their children according to morals and values grounded in biblical principles.

14 15 16 17 18 19 20   /   10 9 8 7 6 5 4 3 2 1

table of contents

Foreword by Gary T. Smalley and Greg Smalley 8

Introduction 10

Session One: The Courtship—Song of Songs 2:13 13
    Just as courtship is an important element in preparing for
    marriage, so it is vital for a loving, growing marriage.

Session Two: The Passion—Song of Songs 1:2 23
    Sexual intimacy is meant to be a celebration of lifelong love
    and commitment between a husband and wife.

Session Three: The Counterfeit—Proverbs 6:27 37
    Faithfulness means staying out of the gray areas and standing
    in the bright white of God's design for marriage.

Session Four: The Great Romance—Zephaniah 3:17 49
    Passion and romance in marriage offer but a glimpse
    of the intense love God has for His bride.

Leader's Discussion Guide 59

foreword

Focus on the Family's *The Family Project* is the largest single initiative in the ministry's history. It is designed to address the question of whether the institutions of marriage and family, as God created them and explains them in Scripture, are still best for human health and happiness. In a day and age when these institutions seem to undergo constant redefinition—and when divorce and the complexities of daily life are taking a devastating toll on marriage and family—we need to ask what God had in mind when He made them in the first place.

The Focus on the Family Marriage Series is a key resource in that initiative. Based on the book *Your Marriage Masterpiece*, this series looks "behind the curtain" of history. Other parts of the program make the case that marriage and family reflect the nature of God Himself; this series looks in greater detail at the many aspects that make up the divine masterwork that is the marriage relationship.

Focus on the Family is well known and respected worldwide for its steadfast dedication to preserving the sanctity of marriage and family life. This series is well written, biblically sound and right on target for guiding couples to explore the foundation God has laid for marriage and to see Him as the role model for the perfect spouse. Through this series, seeds will be planted that will germinate in your heart and mind for many years to come.

In our practical, bottom-line culture, we often want to jump over the *why* and get straight to the *what*. We think that by *doing* the six steps or *learning* the five ways, we will reach the goal. But deep-rooted growth is slower and more purposeful and begins with a well-grounded understanding of God's divine design. Knowing why marriage exists is crucial to making the how-tos more effective. Marriage is a gift from God, a unique and distinct covenant relationship through which His glory and goodness can resonate, and only through knowing the architect and His plan will marriages be built on the surest foundation.

God created marriage; He has a specific purpose for it, and He is committed to filling with fresh life and renewed strength each union yielded to Him. God wants to gather the hearts of every couple together, unite them in love and walk them to the finish line—all in His great grace and goodness.

May God, in His grace, lead you into His truth, strengthening your lives and your marriage.

Gary T. Smalley
Smalley Institute and Bestselling Author

Greg Smalley
Vice President, Family Ministry, Focus on the Family

 introduction

---

At the beginning of creation God "made them male and female." "For this reason a man will leave his father and mother and be united to his wife, and the two will become one flesh." So they are no longer two, but one.
Mark 10:6-8

The Passionate Marriage can be used in a variety of situations, including small-group Bible studies, Sunday School classes, counseling or mentoring situations. A couple can also use this book as an at-home marriage-building study.

Each of the four sessions contains four main components.

Session Overview

Tilling the Ground
This is an introduction to the topic being discussed—commentary and questions to direct your thoughts toward the main idea of the session.

Planting the Seed
This is the Bible study portion in which you will read Scripture and answer questions to help discover lasting truths from God's Word.

Watering the Hope
This is a time for discussion and prayer. Whether you are using the study at home as a couple, in a small group or in a classroom setting, talking about the lesson with your spouse is a great way to solidify the truth and plant it deeply into your hearts.

Harvesting the Fruit
As a point of action, this portion of the session offers suggestions on putting the truth of the Word into action in your marriage relationship.

Suggestions for Individual Couple Study

There are at least three options for using this study as a couple.

- It may be used as a devotional study that each spouse would study individually through the week; then on a specified day, come together and discuss what you have learned and how to apply it to your marriage.
- You might choose to study one session together in an evening and then work on the application activities during the rest of the week.
- Because of the short length of this study, it is a great resource for a weekend retreat. Take a trip away for the weekend, and study each session together, interspersed with your favorite leisure activities.

Suggestions for Group Study

There are many ways that this study can be used in a group situation. The most common way is in a small-group Bible study format. However, it can also be used in an adult Sunday School class. However you choose to use it, there are some general guidelines to follow for group study.

- Keep the group small—five to six couples is probably the maximum.
- Ask couples to commit to regular attendance for the four weeks of the study. Regular attendance is a key to building relationships and trust in a group.
- Encourage participants *not* to share anything of a personal or potentially embarrassing nature without first asking the spouse's permission.
- Whatever is discussed in the group meetings is to be held in strictest confidence among group members only.

There are additional leader helps in the back of this book.

Suggestions for Mentoring or Counseling Relationships

This study also lends itself for use in relationships where one couple mentors or counsels another couple.

- A mentoring relationship could be arranged through a system set up by a church or ministry: A couple that has been married for several years is assigned to meet on a regular basis with a younger couple.
- A less formal way to start a mentoring relationship is for a younger couple to take the initiative and approach a couple that exemplify a mature, godly marriage and ask them to meet with them on a regular basis. Or the reverse might be a mature couple that approaches a younger couple to begin a mentoring relationship.
- When asked to mentor, some might shy away and think that they could never do that, knowing that their own marriage is less than perfect. But just as we are to disciple new believers, we must learn to disciple married couples to strengthen marriages in this difficult world. The Lord has promised to be "with you always" (Matthew 28:20).
- Before you begin to mentor a couple, first complete the study yourselves. This will serve to strengthen your own marriage and prepare you for leading another couple.
- Be prepared to learn as much or more than the couple(s) you will mentor.

The Focus on the Family Marriage Series is based on Al Janssen's The Marriage Masterpiece, *an insightful look at what marriage can—and should—be. In this study, we are pleased to lead you through the wonderful journey of discovering the joy in your marriage that God wants you to experience!*

session one

THE
courtship

Arise, come, my darling; my beautiful one, come with me.
Song of Songs 2:13

Flowers, candy, romantic dinners, phone calls, e-mails, love letters, hours of careful planning, meticulous obsessing, making sure that your feelings of love are clearly communicated to your one and only—developing a relationship with that special someone is an exciting, though sometimes frantic, process.

In light of these grand designs and intense feelings, it is interesting to note how often this courting pursuit wanes after marriage. Is courtship only for before you say "I do"? If not, what part does courtship play in marriage?

The marriage relationship is meant to be a reflection of our divine union with God Himself, and the Bible has some specific instructions about how to develop this intimate joining of lives. The experience of courtship, where friendship and love are cultivated by spending time alone together, does not only lift a relationship off the ground but also keeps it soaring through the sky. Just as your relationship with God is meant to be enjoyed in ever-increasing delight, your marriage is also meant to be savored as a loving, *growing* relationship.

tilling the ground

Loves stories come in all shapes and sizes but can be boiled down to one pursuit: the desire to know and be known—the yearning for intimacy with one special person. This God-given desire is meant to help us reflect upon His own desire for intimate relationship with us.

1. Describe your first date with your spouse. Where did you go? What did you do? How did you feel?

2. What did you most enjoy about being with your spouse while you were still dating?

3. In your opinion, what is the primary purpose of the period of time a couple spends together before they get married?

4. What are some ways you communicated your feelings of love to your spouse before you were married?

5. How did you and your spouse use your courting time to build upon and strengthen your love for each other?

6. What, if anything, would you do differently if you were to relive your courting days?

Dating. Courtship. Marriage. The Bible does much more than merely tell us how to develop strong, intimate relationships: it gives us clear and powerful examples. In this session we're going to hold up our current ideas about courting and marriage against one of the greatest biblical love stories of all time, as told in Song of Songs. It is the story of a Shulamite girl and the king who loved her.

planting the seed

If you were asked to choose a song to represent your marriage, what would that song be? Perhaps you and your spouse already have a special tune, and when the notes of your song find their way to your ears, a sweet smile of remembrance comes sneaking up on you: How beautiful, how romantic, how perfect everything was. Music has a way of planting memories deep in our souls.

In some ways love is a lot like music: it finds its way into our hearts, deeply burrowing its roots to ensure that powerful and enduring attachments will grow and blossom. The love between a man and woman unconditionally committed and truly vulnerable to each other is not a shallow-rooted weed that lasts only until the sun beats down on it. Rather, it is a strong and firmly grounded intimacy anchored to God's unending love. Love is supposed to be amazing—God made it so!

Meet the Happy Couple!

The Song of Songs—also called Song of Solomon—is a poem about the love between a lowly Shulamite girl and the glorious King Solomon. Solomon's Song of Songs is filled with wisdom from God about the love between a husband and wife, based upon Solomon's own love for a small-town girl.

While this poem is often considered to be strictly an allegory of God's love for His people—His Bride—most Bible scholars agree that it is first and foremost an erotic love poem about an actual couple and their experience of married love. It's blushingly open about the passion these two lovebirds felt and how they carried their feelings of intimate love into their marriage, and through these verses we can see that marriage is meant to be a romance. Song of Songs relates God's endorsement of a pure and passionate marriage. Throughout the eight chapters of Song of Songs, two ideas surface as examples of how courtship can—and should—stay alive in marriage.

Mutual Admiration

7. Read the following passages from Song of Songs and note the different ways in which the lovers praise each other:

   1:9-10,15,16

   2:14

   4:1-5,7,9

   5:10-16

   6:4-7

   7:1-6

It doesn't take long to see that Solomon was greatly attracted to his bride. Over and over again, her beauty—both her physical and her inner beauty—is extolled. Likewise, Solomon's bride is enthralled by her husband.

Before marriage, couples are often enamored with the physical features of their intended—she dreams about his cute smile and long eyelashes; he thinks about the way her hair falls softly around her face, and so on. After a period of time, however, partners stop appreciating how beautiful their loved one really is, allowing familiarity to steal the wonder of their initial attraction.

This blindness doesn't have to happen, and in a truly growing marriage relationship, it *shouldn't* happen. Taking a cue from wise Solomon, husbands and wives should continue to praise both the inner and outer beauty of their spouse, keeping those feelings of attraction kindled and glowing.

8. What first attracted you to your spouse?

9. Thinking about your courting days, which of your partner's physical features did you find most attractive?

   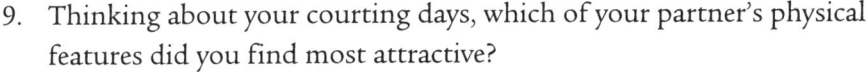

   What are some physical features of your spouse that you find beautiful now?

10. In what ways is your spouse's inner beauty evident to you now?

11. Have you ever written about the attributes of your spouse that you appreciate? Write a brief paragraph, praising him or her.

Words of admiration serve as the fuel that keeps the feelings of attraction and love alive. You were initially attracted to your spouse—and that attraction doesn't have to fade over time. Giving and receiving verbal praise will strengthen the commitment each of you has to your marriage by reaffirming the love you have for each other and declaring each other's worth.

Time Alone—Together

Another important component of a courting marriage is spending time alone together, developing an intimate and meaningful connection. Before marriage, couples make spending time together a high priority, carving out time from their daily routines wherever they can just to see each other.

After marriage, many couples fail to make this time together an ongoing part of their relationship. The busyness of work, community and social commitments can drain energy levels, leaving couples with little motivation to plan yet another thing to do. But alone time with your spouse is far from just another thing to do; it is an essential point of contact that allows for intimacy not only to be maintained but also to be deepened.

Looking at Solomon and his bride, we see how often they speak of getting away by themselves to celebrate their love for each other. Sometimes it is only for moments, sometimes they are away together for days, but in each instance, this loving couple is alone, expressing the fondness and delight they find in being together.

12. Read the following verses from Song of Songs and note which partner in each verse is asking to go away and where the couple is going:

   1:4

   2:10-13

   7:11

   8:14

As difficult as it is for married couples to plan time alone together, we see from the example of Solomon and the Shulamite that alone time is vital to cultivating a passionate relationship. Consider the following questions as they apply to your own marriage:

13. How often do you spend uninterrupted quiet time with your spouse?

    Which of you is most often the one to initiate the alone time you spend as a couple?

    o Me   o My spouse

14. What is the biggest roadblock to planning alone time with your spouse?

    What can you do to get beyond this roadblock?

watering the hope

Consider the story of Mike and Kate.

> Mike and Kate were married several years ago. They met in college, married after they graduated and set up house as a happy and connected couple. As the years passed and life became more complicated, Mike made less of an effort to express his appreciation of Kate's beauty, both as a woman and as his soulmate, and Kate stopped declaring her admiration of Mike's integrity and wisdom as the head of their home.
>
> At a romantic dinner to celebrate their seventh anniversary, Mike and Kate sat at a table, trying to think of things to talk about. They had never considered that their marriage might be in trouble, but now, as they stared blankly at each other, each realized that they had grown apart in many ways.[1]

15. What advice might you give this couple?

16. How much of a role does physical attraction play in courtship and in marriage?

    How much should it play?

17. In what ways are words as powerful as actions when it comes to continually courting your spouse?

18. How has your expression of admiration and love changed since you first met your spouse?

19. To what extent should loving feelings be the basis for courting your spouse after you are married?

20. How can expressing mutual admiration for one another and spending time alone together help couples who no longer feel attracted to their spouses?

After sharing your ideas, spend some time in prayer, asking God to deepen the love you have for your spouse. Pray that He would open your eyes to see your loved one as He does.

harvesting the fruit

Share your answers to questions 8-10 and then take turns reading the paragraphs you wrote in response to question 11.

When you have completed your sharing, pray together, thanking God for the gift of your spouse and what he or she means to you.

Many Bible versions break up the passages in Song of Songs so that the book reads like a script, with "Beloved" (Solomon), "Friends" and "Lover" (the Shulamite) each taking turns speaking.

Make a date this week to spend time reading through Song of Songs with your spouse, speaking aloud the parts of the lover and his bride to each other. As you do, think about the passion and value that this biblical couple expressed for one another, and then discuss how you can express that same type of passion and value to your spouse.

Note
1. This is a compilation of several stories. Any resemblance to an actual situation is purely coincidental.

session two

THE
passion

Let him kiss me with the kisses of his mouth—
for your love is more delightful than wine.
Song of Songs 1:2

Modern culture scoffs at the seemingly rigid biblical boundaries for sexual intimacy; yet society is paying a dear price for its promiscuity. From the staggering casualties of shattered marriages to the rampant spread of sexually transmitted diseases to the millions of aborted babies, it is more and more apparent that God's original plan is worthy of serious consideration.

It shouldn't be surprising that most sexual encounters outside of marriage seldom lead to lasting monogamous relationships. God's Word has been clear all along. "The body is not meant for sexual immorality" (1 Corinthians 6:13). Proverbs 5:15-19 reminds us that sexual relations are exclusively reserved for marriage. It is in the context of marriage that God intended that a couple "will become one flesh" (Genesis 2:24).

tilling the ground

From the very beginning, God's plan has been for every married couple to experience the fullness of romantic love for each other. In a culture that idolizes romance and encourages sexual exploration and experience in any context, it can be hard to understand the mysterious, beautiful expression of love that God originally intended.

1. Thinking of a recent romantic movie, TV show or book that you have viewed or read, how were romance, love and/or sexual intimacy portrayed?

2. How does the world's view of romantic love and sexual intimacy differ from God's view?

3. In your opinion, why did God create sex?

As we observed in the first session of this study, Song of Songs upholds a picture of marital love as it was meant to be. In this love story we find a glimpse of what God intended for marriage—only through the mutually exclusive commitment of a husband and wife can holy and unbridled passion be found. Such authentic love provides for the expression of sexual intimacy in a way that nurtures long-term blessing and fulfillment.

planting the seed

God designed marriage to be a reflection of our union with Him. Therefore, every aspect of a marriage relationship is meant to draw our eyes back to God. When we delve into the topic of sexual intimacy, it can be easy to think that God is not involved—but He is. Sexual intimacy is God's idea, and it is a gift from Him to a husband and wife.

4. Read Proverbs 5:15-19. How does a lifelong commitment between a man and a woman contribute to healthy sexual intimacy?

5. Would there be a difference in sexual intimacy between those who are married and those who are not? Why or why not?

Experiencing true intimacy, trust and vulnerability with your spouse is what makes sex in marriage a special experience unlike that outside of marriage, which is simply a sexual act performed for sexual gratification. The emotions we experience in this total surrender to our spouse give us only a glimpse of the emotional intimacy we can experience as God's chosen Bride.

Defining Intimacy

We all have an innate desire to know and be known. Too often, however, marriage is viewed as a goal and sex is viewed as the ultimate conquest. This ideology shortchanges God's purpose in marriage. Just as the goal of a relationship with God is much greater than securing a place in heaven, the goal of a marriage far exceeds merely making the relationship legal. God calls us to passionate intimacy with Himself *and* with one another.

For many, intimacy is an exotic animal on the safari of life—seldom seen and hard to apprehend. But God, through His Word, shows us that intimacy is a real and vital part of our lives. True intimacy speaks of transparency, a developing trust, a safe place. More often than not, it's assumed that if a couple gets along and engages in sexual relations on a periodic basis, they've arrived at this place called "intimacy"—or at least they've made a visit. However, God's Word teaches that sexual intimacy is about body and soul coming together as one. As much as the world seeks to make this union a purely physical one, Scripture reveals a weaving tapestry of relationship in which the virtues of lifelong love and commitment are celebrated.

6. How do Genesis 1:27-28 and 2:21-24 relate to sexual intimacy?

7. What observations about commitment and intimacy can you make from Genesis 2:24?

Genuine intimacy can be quite intimidating. Consider the admonishment of Paul to the Christians of Ephesus: "Wives, submit to your husbands as to the Lord. Husbands, love your wives, just as Christ loved the church and gave himself up for her" (Ephesians 5:22,25). To many people, including Christians, this sounds more like a prison sentence than a romantic invitation for passionate love. Certainly such implicit trust and sacrifice doesn't fall off trees—or does it?

Growing Intimacy

Sexual intimacy is often portrayed as an effortless delight that just happens when a couple comes together. In reality, busy schedules, drained emotions and daily stress can quickly dampen the fires of romance. Wanting intimacy is one thing; obtaining it is another, requiring sustained effort to achieve. So how can we cultivate and nurture passionate intimacy in our marriages?

First you must ask yourself, *Am I willing to cultivate the soil in order to enjoy the fruit?* True sexual intimacy requires ongoing nurturing in many areas of marriage.

Partnership

If the only consistent time we take a genuine interest in and show appreciation toward our spouse is in our approach to lovemaking, chances are that our spouse will feel used and exploited—and rightly so.

8. How does Ecclesiastes 4:9-12 apply to building a partnership in marriage?

   What are you doing to further create a sense of partnership in the life of your marriage?

9. Do you share a mutual ownership of dreams and ambitions, or is it every one for him- or herself in your relationship? What are you willing to give up to see the dreams of your spouse come true?

Trust and Security

The foundation of growing passion and intimacy are moored in trust and security.

10. What do the following verses say about the importance of trust and security?

    Proverbs 14:1

    Proverbs 17:17

    Proverbs 31:10-11

    Song of Songs 8:6

    Matthew 19:6

    Colossians 3:12-14

11. How does Genesis 2:25 relate to trust and security in marriage?

12. What are you doing now to communicate to your spouse that you are committed to going the distance in your relationship?

    What more do you need to do?

13. How do you respond when challenged to grow in the areas of trust and security?

From the beginning God intended marriage to be a relationship of complete acceptance and total transparency. There is something dangerous about opening ourselves up to another individual—a fear that maybe our loved one won't like us if he or she knows what we are really like. However, Christ calls us to push beyond our fears and embrace true intimacy, for it's there that true sexual oneness and unbridled passion is found.

Reconciliation

If someone is living with unresolved guilt or shame in regard to his or her sexuality, then he or she will most likely view sex through the eyes of fear and/or failure. If a person has been violated or has grown up in an environment where sex was repressed or exploited, it is very possible to view sex as shameful, hurtful or impure. More often than not, sexual wounds distort one's ability to relate to others and inspire behaviors that are self-defeating.

14. According to Romans 12:2; 2 Corinthians 5:17; James 5:16 and 1 John 1:9, what are some ways we can resolve our struggle with guilt, shame and forgiveness?

15. What constructive steps can be taken to reconcile past sexual mistakes while strengthening your moral integrity?

16. What are some other ways to nurture a God-centered perspective of sexuality?

Passionate Intimacy

There are numerous resources available pertaining to the physical aspects of sexual intimacy. Becoming informed of such resources is just the beginning. But the writer of Hebrews 13:4 admonished that "marriage should be honored by all, and the marriage bed kept pure."

But what are the ground rules of sex for a husband and wife? The Bible teaches that sexual intimacy between a husband and wife is to be not only habitual but also mutually satisfying.

17. What does 1 Corinthians 7:4-5 say about the sexual responsibilities of a husband and wife?

What does this mean in the practical realities of daily life?

Sex in marriage is both a responsibility and a privilege, revolving not around one's personal gratification but rather through shared intimacy, as we are reminded in Proverbs 5:18-19: "May your fountain be blessed, and may you rejoice in the wife of your youth. A loving doe, a graceful deer . . . may you ever be captivated by her love."

watering the hope

Consider Kurt and Melinda's story.

> High-school sweethearts Kurt and Melinda were sexually active during most of their junior and senior years. After graduation, as Kurt prepared to go to a college out of state and Melinda made plans to attend the local university, each promised the other that they would keep in touch.
>
> Collegiate lifestyle was more hectic than either Kurt or Melinda had anticipated, and it was only a matter of months before their busy pace had all but swallowed their time and affection for one another.
>
> Melinda did fine for several months, but she wrestled with loneliness from time to time. During the end of her freshman year she was befriended by a couple of Christians who warmly escorted her into a truly caring community of friends, where she dated only occasionally.
>
> In the meantime Kurt continued to date a wide range of women at school, becoming sexually involved with a few. After a disastrous breakup at the end of his senior year, he decided to move back to his hometown to start his career. It wasn't long before Kurt and Melinda ran into each other. Kurt was curious about the change in Melinda, and when she invited him to attend a church service, he gladly went. After attending just a few times, Kurt made a commitment to Christ.
>
> Kurt and Melinda—now both Christians—had a great time getting reacquainted. It was just like the old days. In fact, it was a little too much like the old days, including the physical temptations they faced. Three months after Kurt accepted Christ, he asked Melinda to marry him, and three months later they said their wedding vows in the church where both had accepted Christ.

A few months into their marriage, Kurt and Melinda were perplexed by the growing disconnection in their sex life. Melinda couldn't understand her disinterest while Kurt seemed to be drifting emotionally. Between their jobs, attending church and their social activities, it became too easy to give their attention to other things. As they approached their one-year anniversary, Kurt and Melinda realized they had a problem.[1]

18. What would you say are the key issues that Kurt and Melinda need to face?

   What would you encourage them to do about these issues?

19. What might be intimacy killers in a relationship?

20. What needs of a healthy relationship are neglected when sex is the only emotional expression in a marriage?

harvesting the fruit

21. What expectations do you have for your sex life with your spouse? Have you communicated these expectations to him or her?

22. What actions of your spouse encourage feelings of trust, security, affection, partnership and passion?

   What additional things would also demonstrate love, security and partnership?

23. Are there any unresolved issues such as past sexual abuse, promiscuity, hurtful relationships or fear of abandonment that need to be dealt with before you can experience true intimacy with your spouse? What do you need to do to begin to resolve this issue?

Note: If you have experienced serious problems that are having a detrimental effect on the intimacy in your relationship, we advise you to seek professional help through a reputable Christian counselor. Your pastor may be able to guide you in finding the right person, or you can call Focus on the Family's counseling department (1-800-A-Family or 1-719-531-3400) for a free consultation by a licensed counselor[2] and a referral to a national counseling service network of over 2,000 licensed counselors throughout the United States.

24. What actions or circumstances are passion killers for you?

For your spouse?

Passionate intimacy is not perfect; it is authentic. It is not a destination; it's a journey. It's about imperfect people in an imperfect world giving way to a perfect love.

Passionate intimacy makes allowance for struggles and shortcomings along the way, yet it is committed to a path of personal growth and maturity, unrelenting in its pursuit of a real, healthy relationship. Our desire to extend love begins to outweigh our longing to be loved. It empowers us to face our relational pain and disappointment in order to experience God's healing touch. Such love is not self-centered but God-centered. It is this passionate intimacy that reflects the intimate love of God's divine romance with humanity.

After this discussion on intimacy and passion, you may need to spend some time in prayer with and for each other. Take time to ask forgiveness of your spouse for past hurts or disappointments and to extend that forgiveness to your spouse. Thank God for your spouse and for your relationship, asking Him to bless your marriage with increasing intimacy.

Bonus: *Considering what you have learned about your spouse's needs, make a list of things that you can do that especially express love and trust to your spouse. Plan what you will do every day during the next week—and into the following weeks—to demonstrate your love in ways that are most meaningful to your spouse.*

Notes
1. This is a compilation of several stories. Any resemblance to an actual situation is purely coincidental.
2. Counselors at Focus on the Family are licensed in the state of Colorado.

session three

THE
counterfeit

Can a man scoop fire into his lap without his clothes being burned?
Proverbs 6:27

Have you ever reasoned with yourself regarding *harmless* flirtations with infidelity? Let's take a look into the mind of someone trying to justify this type of behavior.

> *It's harmless, right? I steal an extended gaze at an attractive coworker. No one sees as I enjoy a fleeting fantasy of what life would be like if we were together. No one knows as I give a flirty—but harmless!—compliment. No one gets hurt—why, it actually helps me be a better partner! It keeps my life exciting which, in turn, keeps my marriage more exciting. What does it matter as long as I don't actually do anything?*

It is easy to see how the boundary line of fidelity can become hazy. There is so little black and white in this world, so few points where our collective conscience stands united as to what is right and what is wrong. And nowhere is this line more apt to turn gray than in our relationships. Driven by the desire for personal happiness, we have an avalanche of opinion saying that we should do whatever we need to do to be happy.

What exactly is infidelity, anyway? To begin with, infidelity is much more than having an affair—it is an issue of the heart attitude. If you are going to deepen your marriage relationship and experience intimacy as God intended, you must consider what it means to be faithful. Leaning on God's Word and His example as the foundation of true faithfulness, you can learn ways to strengthen your marriage commitment—staying out of the gray areas and standing in the bright white of God's divine design for marriage.

tilling the ground

Newspaper and tabloid headlines reflect the ongoing saga of unfaithfulness in society today. It is often the theme of many movies or TV shows as well.

1. Thinking about the past month, how many times would you estimate that you have read or heard about marital breakups due to infidelity?

2. What current movies, TV shows or songs can you think of that show the attractiveness or acceptability of unfaithfulness?

   Which ones portray the negative side of infidelity?

3. In your opinion, is infidelity more of an attitude or an action? Why?

4. Is sexual exclusivity important? Why or why not?

By and large, our culture rejects the idea that sexual intimacy is reserved exclusively for marriage. Just take a look at a top-40 song list or scroll through the TV channels and you'll see countless voices glorifying feel-good, please-yourself lifestyles.

Taking a closer look at God's Word reveals that His intention for the physical union between a man and a woman in marriage is more than a physical act; it is where true intimacy is established and nurtured. True faithfulness to our spouse occurs only when we selfishly guard this place of genuine intimacy, avoiding wandering into the gray zone of seemingly harmless thoughts and actions.

planting the seed

When we consider examples of marital faithfulness, we don't often think of God. Yet He is an example not only of true faithfulness but also of right responses to unfaithfulness. He has borne the brunt of infidelity and spousal rejection over and over again. Though bound to Him by covenant, God's chosen people rejected Him many times for other gods and earthly kings.

What motivates people to wander away from their marriage promises? Exactly how important is fidelity? If God, the consummate example of faithfulness, was deserted by His Bride, is there any hope that any marriage might navigate the choppy waters of temptation without crashing into the rocks of infidelity? Gladly, the answer to this question is a resounding YES!

What Is Fidelity?

Very simply, faithfulness, or fidelity, means letting our actions match up with our words. Being faithful means keeping our promises; we can be counted upon to do what we say we will do. Faithful people are dependable, loyal and steadfast.

Society tends to define unfaithfulness by the law, asserting that if there is no physical or romantic love involved in one's actions, then there is no unfaithfulness. But infidelity isn't just a physical act or romantic interlude—infidelity begins in the heart. In a marriage relationship, being faithful means that you adhere to your promise for an exclusive, intimate relationship with your spouse—an exclusivity that touches upon all aspects of your being, from your mind to your body to your soul. When this foundation is weakened because someone else has been allowed into this intimate circle, the covenant has been violated and the promises have been broken.

5. As you read the following verses from Song of Songs, note what each says about the exclusiveness of the marriage commitment:

   2:16

   6:3

   7:10

Infidelity is allowing your heart to be drawn away from your mate. Anytime you place your devotion or affection in someone other than your spouse you are, in effect, being unfaithful and setting your marriage up for failure. Marital exclusivity mirrors the same type of devotion God desires for us to share with Him. Since marriage is a reflection of our union with the Lord, it follows that both our devotion to Him and to our spouse should be exclusive and steadfast.

How Does Infidelity Start?

If infidelity is rooted in wandering away from the marriage promise, then it must begin as an act of the heart. Entertaining improper thoughts is the first step on the road to adultery. We often justify compromising choices, not realizing that each excuse is leading us further and further away from the protection of the covenant we share with God and with our spouse.

6. In James 1:14-15, what is the progression from temptation to sin?

7. According to Romans 8:5-6, how does our mind-set affect our lifestyle?

8. What did Jesus say about adultery in Matthew 5:27-30?

9. Many people feel adultery is wrong but see nothing wrong with lust, as long as one doesn't act on it. What is your opinion?

In our sex-saturated society, many people set their thoughts on culturally accepted reasons for infidelity. They become fooled by their feelings and justify their wrong choices with excuses: *I made a mistake. I married the wrong person. I know I'm married, but I've never felt this way about anyone, not even my spouse. This must be* true *love.* These subtle thoughts can wreak havoc in a marriage.

10. What are some reasons you have heard people use to justify infidelity?

11. In your opinion, when does unfaithfulness begin?

What Does Infidelity Falsely Promise?

We began this study by looking at the passionate marriage between the wisest man on Earth, Solomon, and his lovely bride, the Shulamite woman. They had a vibrant, satisfying relationship that serves as a model for all marriages. But somewhere along the road, Solomon got off track and allowed his passionate devotion to become polluted by false intimacy and infidelity. Instead of enjoying the rich marriage relationship he once had, his unfaithfulness ended his marriage and he spent the remainder of his life miserable and lonely.

12. What are Solomon's observations in Ecclesiastes 2:1-2,8,10-11 about getting everything that he wanted?

   How do these verses apply to fidelity/infidelity in marriage?

Infidelity promises satisfaction and fulfillment. But is that what it *really* gives? Rather than providing ongoing satisfaction and peace, infidelity leaves in its wake brokenness and despair. Why? Because true intimacy can only be enjoyed within the confines of an exclusive covenant relationship. Marriage is meant to be enjoyed between one man and one woman, and to bring another into that union denies the nature of that union itself.

13. How does Jesus describe marriage in Matthew 19:5-6?

14. Summarize 1 Corinthians 6:13,15-16. What does it mean to "become one flesh"?

    What are the implications of this union?

15. Why do you think sexual sin is unlike other sins? (See 1 Corinthians 6:18.)

16. Summarize Solomon's advice in each of the following passages:

    Proverbs 5:3-4

    Proverbs 6:25-29

Breaking your marriage promise to your spouse, whether in thought or by action, is a betrayal of confidence and a breach of the covenant. As husband and wife, you are joined by the Lord to mirror the oneness He desires to have with His creation. Guarding your marriage is vital in allowing God to use you as a witness of His amazing love to others.

How Can Infidelity Be Avoided?

The Bible gives us definite guidelines for walking along the road of covenant marriage. We begin by becoming accountable for our thoughts and actions.

Reading the Bible, praying alone and with others, and being connected to other believers are all essential parts of accountability. Yet, even with these things in place, there will come a time when you will be faced with a strong temptation to be unfaithful. When this happens, remember that God is with you and has promised to help.

17. Summarize what the following verses say about building accountability:

    Proverbs 13:20

    Galatians 6:2

    Hebrews 10:24-25

    James 5:16

18. Read 1 Corinthians 10:13. What do you think "a way out" means?

The safest guard against unfaithfulness is to realize that it *is* possible for you to choose it—or not. Once you are aware of this, you can keep your heart and mind guarded against thoughts that draw you away from your marriage covenant.

What If I've Already Failed?

To some degree, we have all failed in keeping our hearts fully faithful to our spouse. What do we do to get ourselves back on track and enjoying the true intimacy of a marriage covenant?

Repent

Read Ephesians 5:3,8,11. The mandate from God is clear: If we are His children, then we must live lives that glorify Him. When we repent, we purposefully change our thoughts and actions from that which we know is wrong and start going in the opposite direction.

If you have started down the road of infidelity—no matter how far it has taken you—stop! Consider what the consequences will be. Remember that marriage is a divine union, a covenant meant to last a lifetime. And it is *not* too late for you to reclaim the marriage God intended.

Accept God's Forgiveness

Read 1 John 1:9-10. Jesus can restore us to full fellowship with God. This does not mean that sin is overlooked or ignored; it means that the grace of God has reached in to our dark and sinful lives with freedom and forgiveness. Jesus took the punishment for our sins upon Himself. He paid the price at Calvary, and though it will take time, the healing He offers can restore broken hearts and broken marriages.

Make a Commitment to Purity

Read Colossians 3:1-17. Allowing others who are mature and wise to advise and correct you is the infrastructure of accountability. These are the people who will help you deal with the betrayal, heal the wounds and walk through the restoration process. Place yourself under the spotlight, where healing can begin.

Infidelity is something everyone has to deal with one way or another because it is much more than a physical act. It is a breach of the spiritual covenant we have made before God with our spouse. Even happily married couples struggle with the temptation of infidelity from time to time. The key is in holding yourself accountable to God and to your spouse so that those temptations can be resisted and overcome.

watering the hope

Read the following story and think about where infidelity begins:

> Jose and Maria had been married for four years. When Paul, a mutual friend of theirs, began to pay compliments to Maria, she laughed and didn't think much of it.
>
> As the weeks went by, Maria seemed to run into Paul more and more, and each time their paths crossed, they talked a little longer. Maria was flattered by the attention but something didn't seem right. She knew she should put a stop to their friendship but she reasoned with herself that they were *only* friends and that nothing they were doing was wrong.
>
> Maria dismissed the uneasiness; then one night, as she and Paul were about to leave a store, she dropped her car keys. When they both reached down to pick them up, Paul's hand landed on Maria's and he leaned over and kissed her. As they stood up, Maria stared at Paul, speechless. Before she knew it, Paul leaned over and kissed her again.
>
> Maria quickly grabbed her keys and went to her car.[1]

19. What should Maria do at this point?

20. Were Maria's actions showing faithfulness to her husband? Why or why not?

21. What actions could Maria have taken to safeguard her marriage commitment?

22. Why is it important to guard the exclusive physical intimacy of marriage?

harvesting the fruit

We've looked at what it means to be faithful in the context of our marriage promise, and we've also considered the consequences of marital infidelity.

23. What safeguards have you set in place to make your marriage affair-resistant?

This next week, read together through the story of Hosea and Gomer in the Old Testament book of Hosea. When you've finished, come up with more safeguards for your marriage and commit to diligently guarding your relationship.

> Spend time in prayer, asking God to reveal areas of potential weakness in your marriage relationship. Ask for His wisdom to strengthen those areas. Pray for God's faithfulness to be worked into your own lives and marriage union.

Note
1. This is a compilation of several stories. Any resemblance to an actual situation is purely coincidental.

session four

THE
great romance

He will take great delight in you, he will quiet you with his love,
he will rejoice over you with singing.
Zephaniah 3:17

Have you ever thought about why classic love stories are so appealing? Something inside people yearns for this kind of romance to be true: Boy and girl meet, fall in love, weather the obstacles of life together and live happily and passionately ever after.

Think for a moment about Solomon and his bride, and the deep attraction and joy they felt in loving each other. Their pure desire and passion for one another sound a call to all couples to enjoy such rich and fulfilling love. We long for this kind of intimate relationship because romance and intimacy are God's idea.

There is a further idea to consider. Song of Songs affirms that the desire for romance is good—but is this romance limited to our spouse? Before we complete this study, let's consider marriage as the union that reflects God's desire for intimacy with us. Marriage is not the end result of a relationship; it is the beginning of one. Through marriage, we can come to understand the kind of intense desire and passion God feels for us, His Bride. God wants us to revel in His love just as the Shulamite woman did in Solomon's love.

Now wait a minute! It's one thing to think about the passion and romance we have with our spouse. It's quite another to think of romance and connect it to our relationship with God. Can God really feel for us what a husband does for his bride? Read on and let God speak for Himself.

tilling the ground

Romance means a lot of things to a lot people. It is a beautiful and fulfilling gift from God meant to be enjoyed between a husband and a wife. But the feelings of romance are also meant to draw our eyes to the intense love that God has for us.

1. What is romance?

2. How important are one's feelings to romance?

3. Think of some couples you know. How do their relationships demonstrate true romance?

   How do these relationships not demonstrate true romance?

4. What is the most romantic thing that your spouse has done for you?

   Let's examine God's model for romance.

planting the seed

We were made to experience intimacy, yet marriage is the foretaste of an even more deeply fulfilling union. The bond we share with God as His Bride is even greater than that which we share with our spouse, and the feelings of love and fulfillment we experience in our marriage point toward a grander fulfillment in God.

The Template for Romance

The concept of God as husband can be seen in the Old Testament (see Isaiah 54:5; Jeremiah 31:32), but one of the clearest passages comes from the New Testament book of Ephesians. The following passage provides the basis for our understanding of marriage as a picture of Christ and His Church.

5. Read Ephesians 5:22-32. What strikes you most about verse 32?

6. What does this passage show you about the ultimate purpose of marriage?

7. How do these instructions about marriage call out to a higher union between Christ and His Church?

God's Love for Us

Is it awkward to think of God's passionate love for His people? Most of us would answer yes. The question is why? Part of the problem is that we have distanced God through our traditions and theology, relegating Him to ruling the universe but not pouring His passion over us as individuals. God is the consummate and sovereign King of all that exists. He sits upon His throne and governs nations with justice and power, but it is His passionate love for His Bride that moves His heart.

8. Read the following passages and summarize how God feels about His people:

    Isaiah 54:10

    Jeremiah 31:3

    Hosea 11:8

    Zephaniah 3:17

Our Love for God

How should we respond to God's deep desire for us? Our eyes should be drawn to Him in hopeful, joyful surrender. We have a heavenly husband who is madly in love with us and longs to pour His love over us.

9. Write the word in each passage that describes how God's people feel about Him.

    Job 19:27

    Psalm 42:1-2

    Psalm 61:4

Psalm 63:1

Psalm 84:2

When Divine Romance Doesn't Make Sense

A divine romance sounds good, doesn't it? But sometimes we just can't make the connection that God passionately pours out His love to us, rejoicing over us as a husband over his bride (see Zephaniah 3:17). We know that God loves us, but we sometimes find it hard to believe He is *passionate* about us. Why? What hinders us from realizing this foundational biblical truth?

Looking Through the Wrong End of the Telescope

Have you ever looked through the wrong end of a telescope or pair of binoculars? Instead of bringing an object closer for viewing, the distance between you and the object is highly exaggerated. Likewise, our perception of our divine romance with God can become deceivingly distanced through our own misunderstanding of His Word. We accept our limited ideas of God's love and fail to look at what He has said and revealed to us.

10. In Exodus 20:5; 34:14; Joshua 24:19 and 1 Corinthians 10:22, what is the common word used to describe how God feels about His people?

    What does this word mean to you, and why would God use it to describe His feelings toward His people?

The word "jealous" is usually used in a negative way, but in its purest form, jealousy is a statement of love and protection. Sin has tainted our ability to love purely so that many times human jealousy is an ungodly response. But this shouldn't discount what jealousy really is: a passionate cry for single-hearted devotion grounded in a covenant relationship. God desires us, His Bride, with passionate jealousy.

Such passion underscores how intimately God loves us. He is not distant; He is closer than we can fathom. When we cannot see this, it is not because He has distanced Himself; it is because we are looking at Him through the wrong end of the telescope.

Living with the Wounds of the Past

Another reason we find it hard to buy in to the idea of a divine romance between ourselves and God is that we are wounded by past disappointments and failures.

Abandonment, rejection and fear have crossed all of our lives at some point. The way in which we navigated through painful experiences directly influences our ability to trust in anyone, including God. After all, if the people we have loved have failed us, how can we know that God won't eventually bail out too? So we hold ourselves at a distance to avoid being hurt. This thinking and mistrust not only hinders us from experiencing the intensity of God's love but also affects our relationships with each other.

The only way to combat these feelings of fear and mistrust is to seek the Lord and to allow the truth of His faithfulness to make us feel secure and whole.

11. As you read the following Scriptures, note what they say about how God feels about you:

    Psalm 117:2

    Isaiah 30:18

    1 Peter 5:7

12. What hinders you the most from believing that God is passionately in love with you?

13. What, if any, connection do you see between your ability to receive God's love and your ability to give God's love to others?

watering the hope

Consider the following story about Paul and Joanne:

> Joanne grew up with a clear understanding of God's love for her as an individual. She rejoiced at feeling deeply loved by Him, so when she married Paul, she had no trouble expressing her joy in giving and receiving love from her new husband.
>
> Paul, however, grew up in a single-parent home with only sporadic contact with his father. As a result, he rarely enjoyed the comfort of feeling unconditionally loved. He never viewed God as being passionate about him as an individual, thinking instead of God only as a distant, powerful king.
>
> It wasn't until after Paul and Joanne married that their polar-opposite concepts clashed. Paul believed that emotions were secondary to commitment and responsibility in building a solid marriage. Joanne believed that marriage was meant to be the fullest human expression of intimacy and a mirror to the kind of love that God has for His Bride. Joanne wanted to share a deep, intimate love with her husband, sustained by ongoing romance and soul-knitting surrender

to each other; Paul was content to live without such dangerous emotions and didn't know why Joanne was getting frustrated.[1]

14. How would you encourage Paul and Joanne?

15. How has your understanding of God's love for you helped shape the way you express love to your spouse?

16. Is it difficult for you to think of God as a passionate husband? Why or why not?

17. How does romance factor in to your relationship with God?

18. What words would you use to best describe God's love for you?

What words best describe your love for your spouse?

harvesting the fruit

19. In what ways have you been looking through the wrong end of the telescope in your relationship with God and in your marriage?

20. In what ways have you been jealous in guarding your marriage relationship?

21. What past relationship wounds are hindering your present relationship with God and with your spouse?

22. How has God demonstrated His love in your marriage?

23. How has your spouse demonstrated unconditional love toward you?

> Take time right now to thank your spouse for the ways he or she has shown love to you. Spend a few moments in prayer, surrendering your past, present and future to the One who made you and loves you with an everlasting love. Affirm your love for one another and ask for God's unconditional love to flow into you and through your relationship to others.

During the coming week, review together each of the verses you've read in this session that describe God's love for His people, and choose one verse to memorize. (You might consider eventually adding all of these verses to your memory banks—for those times when you need to be reminded of His love.)

As you think upon your chosen verse, let the Holy Spirit plant the seeds of truth deep inside your soul: You are loved by God and created to enjoy an intimate union with Him. Understanding how fully and completely He loves you will enhance your ability to romance your spouse and will free you to enjoy marriage as God intended.

Note
1. This is a compilation of several stories. Any resemblance to an actual situation is purely coincidental.

LEADER'S
discussion guide

General Guidelines

1. If at all possible, the group should be led by a married couple. This does not mean that both spouses need to be leading the discussions; perhaps one spouse is better at facilitating discussions while the other is better at relationship building or organization—but the leader couple should share responsibilities wherever possible.
2. At the first meeting, be sure to lay down the ground rules for discussions, stressing that following these rules will help everyone feel comfortable during discussion times.
   a. No one should share anything of a personal or potentially embarrassing nature without first asking his or her spouse's permission.
   b. Whatever is discussed in the group meetings is to be held in strictest confidence among group members only.
   c. Allow everyone in the group to participate. However, as a leader, don't force anyone to answer a question if he or she is reluctant. Be sensitive to the different personalities and communication styles among your group members.
3. Fellowship time is very important in building small-group relationships. Providing beverages and/or light refreshments either before or after each session will encourage a time of informal fellowship.
4. Most people live very busy lives; respect the time of your group members by beginning and ending meetings on time.

How to Use the Material

1. Each session has more than enough material to cover in a 45-minute teaching period. You will probably not have time to discuss every single question in each session, so prepare for each meeting by selecting questions you feel are most important to address for your group; discuss other questions as time permits. Be sure to save the last 10 minutes of your meeting time for each couple to interact individually and to pray together before adjourning.

   Optional Eight-Session Plan—You can easily divide each session into two parts if you'd like to cover all of the material presented in each session. Each section of the session has enough questions to divide in half, and the Bible study sections (Planting the Seed) are divided into two or three sections that can be taught in separate sessions.

2. Each spouse should have his or her own copy of the book in order to personally answer the questions. The general plan of this study is that the couples complete the questions at home during the week and then bring their books to the meeting to share what they have learned during the week.

   However, the reality of leading small groups in this day and age is that some members will find it difficult to do the homework. If you find that to be the case with your group, consider adjusting the lessons and having members complete the study during your meeting time as you guide them through the lesson. If you use this method, be sure to encourage members to share their individual answers with their spouses during the week (perhaps on a date night).

Session One | The Courtship

> *A Note to Leaders:* This Bible study series is based on The Marriage Masterpiece *by Al Janssen. We highly recommend that you read chapters 14 and 15 in preparation for leading this study.*

Before the Meeting

1. Gather materials for making name tags (if couples do not already know each other and/or if you do not already know everyone's name). Also gather extra pens or pencils and Bibles to use as loaners for anyone who needs them.
2. Provide 3x5-inch index cards for recording prayer requests.
3. Read through your own answers and mark the ones that you especially want to have the group discuss.
4. Prepare slips of paper with the references for the verses that you will want someone to read aloud during the sessions. You can pass out these slips as members arrive, but be sensitive to those who are uncomfortable reading aloud or who might not be familiar with the Bible.

Ice Breakers

1. If this is the first time this couples group has met together, have everyone introduce themselves and tell a little bit about the amount of time they have been married, where they were married, etc.
2. Invite couples to share about their first date (question 1).
3. **Option 1:** Ask for two volunteer couples who will answer a few questions about their first date. Have the men leave the room before you ask the women the following questions:
   a. Where did you and your husband meet?
   b. How long after you first met did you have your first date?
   c. Did your husband ask you out first or did you ask him out first?
   d. Where did you go, and what did you do on your first date?

e. Rate that first date on a scale of 1 to 5 (1 = I never wanted to see him again; 5 = It was wonderful; I knew he was the one).

Have someone write down the answers. Bring the husbands back in and ask them the same questions; see how closely they match the wives' answers. Have some fun with this. Perhaps provide a fun, inexpensive prize for the couple who got the most correct answers.

4. **Option 2:** Have couples share if they have a favorite song as a couple. Invite them to share the title and a few of the lyrics with the whole group. If there is time, ask them to share why it is their song.

Discussion

1. **Tilling the Ground**—Invite volunteers to share their answers to questions 3 through 6. (Be sensitive to the time, as you will want to spend most of your discussion time on the next two sections: the Bible study and application.)
2. **Planting the Seed**—If you didn't do option 2 for the ice breaker, invite couples to share what song—if any—is their song and why it is special to them. Lead the group through the Bible study discussion of questions 7-8, 12-14, briefly reviewing the commentary as transitions between the questions.
3. **Watering the Hope**—The case study and questions in this section will help members bring the Bible study into the reality of their own expectations versus God's plan. Don't neglect this part of the study, as it brings the whole lesson into the here and now, applying God's Word to daily life.
4. **Harvesting the Fruit**—This section is meant to help the individual couples apply the lesson to their own marriages and can be dealt with in several ways.
   a. Allow the couples one-on-one time at the end of the meeting. This would require space for them to be alone, with enough space between couples to allow for quiet, private conversations.

   If couples have already answered the questions individually, now would be the time to share their answers. Give a time limit, emphasizing that their discussions can be continued at home if they are not able to answer all of the questions in the time allotted.

If couples have not answered the questions before the meeting, have them answer them together now. This works best when there is open-ended time for the couples to stay until they have completed their discussion and will require that the leaders stay until the last couple has finished.
   b. Instruct couples to complete this section at home during the week after the meeting. This will give them quiet and private time to deal with any issues that might come up and to spend all the time needed to complete the discussion. You will want to follow up at the next meeting to hold couples accountable for completing this part of the lesson.
   c. At times it might be advantageous to pair up two couples to discuss these questions. This would help in building accountability into the study.
5. **Close in Prayer**—An important part of any small-group relationship is the time spent in prayer for one another. This may also be done in a number of ways.
   a. Have couples write out their specific prayer requests on the index cards. These requests may then be shared with the whole group or traded with another couple as prayer partners for the week. If requests are shared with the whole group, pray as a group before adjourning the meeting; if requests are traded, allow time for the prayer-partner couples to pray together.
   b. Gather the whole group together and lead couples in guided prayer.
   c. Have individual couples pray together.

After the Meeting

1. **Evaluate**—Leaders should spend time evaluating the meeting's effectivenes.
2. **Encourage**—During the week, try to contact each couple (through phone calls, notes of encouragement or e-mail/instant messaging) and welcome them to the group. Make yourself available for answering any questions or concerns they may have and generally get to know them. This contact might best be done by the husband-leader contacting the men and the wife-leader contacting the women.

3. **Equip**—Complete the Bible study, even if you have previously gone through this study together.
4. **Pray**—Prayerfully prepare for the next meeting, praying for each couple and for your own preparation.

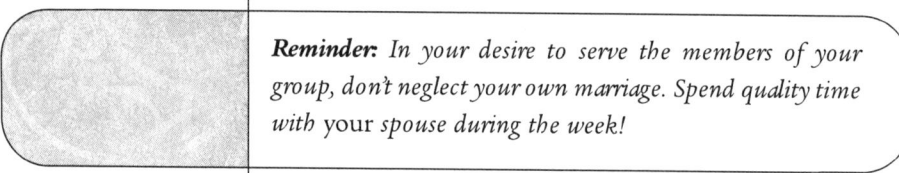

Reminder: *In your desire to serve the members of your group, don't neglect your own marriage. Spend quality time with your spouse during the week!*

Session Two | The Passion

Before the Meeting

1. Gather several Bibles, pens or pencils, and the materials needed to make name tags.
2. Provide 3x5-inch index cards for recording prayer requests.
3. Read through your own answers and mark the ones that you especially want to have the group discuss.
4. Prepare slips of paper with the references for the verses that you will want someone to read aloud during the session. (You can distribute these slips as members arrive.)
5. Gather examples of popular movies, TV shows, music or books that portray romantic themes. This might be in the form of advertisements, reviews, ratings or listings. Or ask each couple to bring in one example of the culture's view of sexual intimacy.

Ice Breakers

1. Distribute index cards and ask members to at least write down their names, even if they don't have specific prayer requests. This way, another couple can pray for them during the up-coming week. (After all, just because we don't have a specific request, it doesn't mean we don't need prayer!)
2. **Option 1:** Display the examples of the movies, TV shows, etc. Discuss how these are different or similar to what God intends for sexual intimacy.
3. **Option 2:** Invite volunteers to share their answers to questions 1 and 2.

Discussion

1. **Tilling the Ground**—Discuss question 3.
2. **Planting the Seed**— Discuss the questions.
3. **Watering the Hope**—Read the case study and then have each couple

pair up with another couple to discuss the questions. If there is time, have the small groups share their answers to question 18.
4. **Harvesting the Fruit**—Have spouses pair up and share their answers to questions 21-24. Be aware of any couples who might have difficulty regarding question 23. Be prepared with names of counselors who can help couples work through these serious issues. These types of problems are not easily resolved without professional help.
5. **Close in Prayer**—Have individual couples pray together following the direction at the end of the session. As members leave, have them select someone else's prayer request card so that they can pray for that person during the coming week.

After the Meeting

1. **Evaluate.**
2. **Encourage** members to call the person for whom they are praying this week.
3. **Equip.**
4. **Pray.**

Session Three | The Counterfeit

Before the Meeting

1. Gather index cards, pens or pencils, and Bibles, as needed.
2. Provide 3x5-inch index cards for recording prayer requests.
3. Read through your own answers and mark the ones that you especially want to have the group discuss.
4. Prepare slips of paper with the references for the verses that you will want someone to read aloud during the session. (You can distribute these slips as members arrive.)
5. Be on the lookout for newspaper or magazine headlines and stories that describe marital breakups due to infidelity. Display these around the meeting room.

Ice Breakers

1. Begin the meeting by inviting couples to share some of the safeguards that they presently have in place for protecting the sanctity of their marriage.
2. Pointing to the examples posted around the room, invite members to respond to questions 1-3 in the Tilling the Ground section.

Discussion

1. **Tilling the Ground**—Discuss question 4.
2. **Planting the Seed**—Discuss the questions. Be alert to anyone in the group who might be dealing with the issue of infidelity—past or present.
3. **Watering the Hope**—Divide the group by gender and have them read the case study and discuss the questions.
4. **Harvesting the Fruit**—Have individual couples pray together.
5. **Close in Prayer**—Have each couple partner with another to share what each has written on his or her prayer request card. Once they've shared, have them pray together.

After the Meeting

1. **Evaluate.**
2. **Encourage** the prayer-partner couples to contact one another during the week to share answers to prayer.
3. **Equip.**
4. **Pray.**

Session Four | The Great Romance

Before the Meeting

1. Provide pens or pencils and Bibles, as needed.
2. Provide 3x5-inch index cards for recording prayer requests.
3. Read through your own answers and mark the ones that you especially want to have the group discuss.
4. Prepare slips of paper with the references for the verses that you will want someone to read aloud during the session. (You can distribute these slips as members arrive.)
5. Gather two sheets of poster board and felt-tip pens. To speed the activity along, you might want to provide a list of romantic couples (e.g., Romeo and Juliet, Scarlett and Rhett, Ruth and Boaz, Sarah and Abraham, Isaac and Rebekah, Duke of Windsor and Wallis Simpson, Caesar and Cleopatra, Humphrey Bogart and Lauren Bacall, Paul Newman and Joanne Woodward, George Burns and Gracie Allen, Buttercup and Westley, George and Martha Washington, Ronald and Nancy Reagan, Jimmy and Roslynn Carter, Billy and Ruth Graham, James and Shirley Dobson).

Ice Breakers

1. Form two groups by gender. Have each group make a list of the 10 most romantic couples—fictional and historical—and rank them, with number 1 being the most romantic. Have them record their lists on the poster board.
2. Have the groups share their lists and why they chose the number one couple. It will be fun to compare the men's list and the women's list.

Discussion

1. **Tilling the Ground**—Discuss questions 1 and 2. If there is time, have volunteers briefly share their response to question 4.
2. **Planting the Seed**—Discuss the questions.
3. **Watering the Hope**—Have each couple partner with another to discuss this section's questions.
4. **Harvesting the Fruit**—Have individual couples share together.
5. **Close in Prayer**—Ask group members to stand in a circle. Invite couples to share one thing that they have learned during this session that has really helped them to grow in their marriage relationship. Close with members offering sentence prayers of praise and worship and then sing a worship song together.

After the Meeting

1. **Evaluate**— Share the importance of feedback, and ask members to take the time this week to write a review of the group meetings and then to return them to you.
2. **Encourage**— Call each couple during the next week and invite them to join you for the next study in the *Focus on the Family Marriage Series*.

Notes

Notes

Notes

Notes

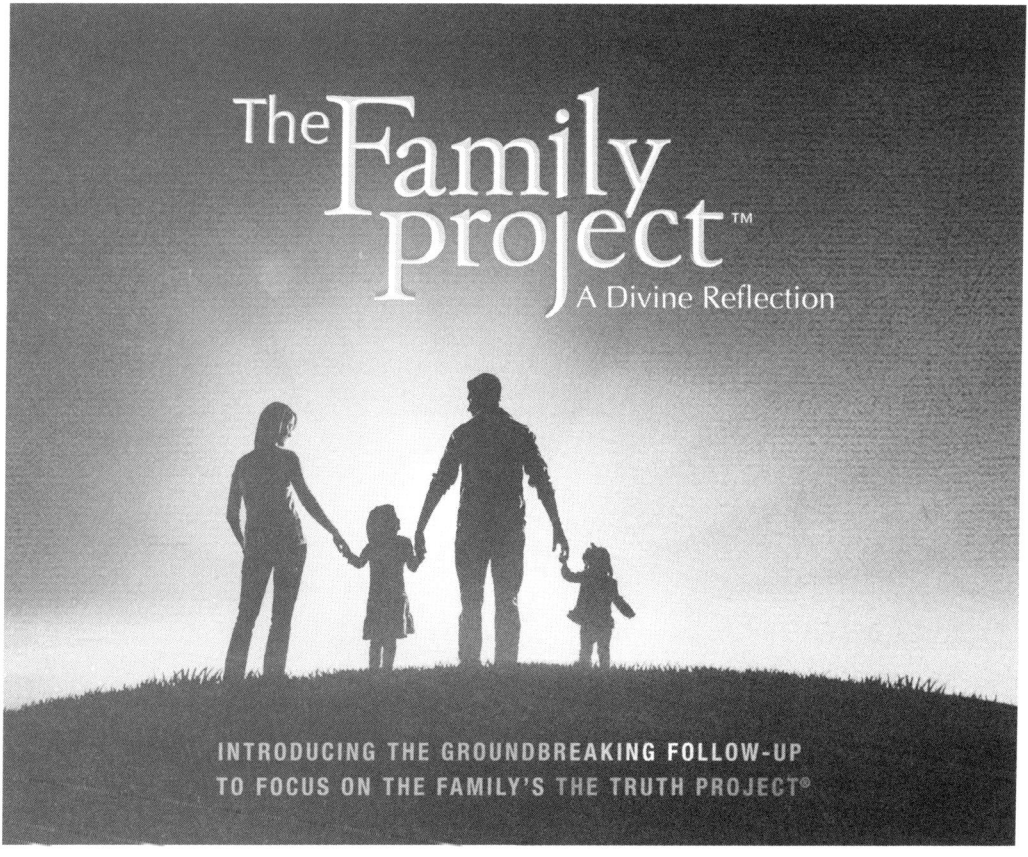

THE PROFOUND IMPACT OF BIBLICAL FAMILIES

From the creators of the life-changing series *Focus on the Family's The Truth Project* comes a stunning, new journey of discovery that explores family as a revelation of God—and the extraordinary impact families have on the world around them. Introducing *The Family Project*, a transformative feature-length documentary and DVD small-group experience that reveals—through an in-depth exploration of God's design and purpose—biblical truths about the role of families in society.

VISIT
FamilyProject.com
TO LEARN MORE

A PROGRAM OF FOCUS ON THE FAMILY

More titles in **The Marriage Series**
from **Focus on the Family**

Each study contains four sessions with four main components:
Tilling the Ground • Planting the Seed • Watering the Hope • Harvesting the Fruit

The Abundant Marriage
Discover God's Extravagant Plan
for Your Life Together
978.07642.16589

The Blended Marriage
Learn How to Cultivate a
Fruitful Life Together
978.07642.16626

The Communicating Marriage
Learn How Open Expression
Strengthens Your Life Together
978.07642.16664

The Covenant Marriage
Discover How God's Promises
Shape Your Life Together
978.07642.16671

The Fighting Marriage
Learn Healthy Ways to Resolve
Conflict in Your Life Together
978.07642.16725

Available wherever books are sold

Focus on the Family is a global Christian ministry dedicated to helping families thrive. They provide help and resources for couples to build healthy marriages that reflect God's design and for parents to raise their children according to morals and values grounded in biblical principles.

More titles in **The Marriage Series**
from **Focus on the Family**

Each study contains four sessions with four main components:
Tilling the Ground • Planting the Seed • Watering the Hope • Harvesting the Fruit

The Giving Marriage
Discover How to Reflect the Love
of Christ in Your Life Together
978.07642.16794

The Masterpiece Marriage
Discover God's Grand Design
for Your Life Together
978.07642.16824

The Model Marriage
Discover the Power of Sacrificial
Love in Your Life Together
978.07642.16848

The Passionate Marriage
Learn How Intimacy Shapes
Your Life Together
978.07642.16862

The Surprising Marriage
Discover the Adventure of
Faith in Your Life Together
978.07642.16909

Available wherever books are sold

 Focus on the Family is a global Christian ministry dedicated to helping families thrive. They provide help and resources for couples to build healthy marriages that reflect God's design and for parents to raise their children according to morals and values grounded in biblical principles.